Pioneers of Science and Discovery

Alfred Nobel
Pioneer of High Explosives

Trevor I. Williams

PRIORY PRESS LIMITED

Other Books in this Series

Carl Benz and the Motor Car   Doug Nye
George Eastman and the Early Photographers   Brian Coe
Richard Arkwright and Cotton Spinning   Richard L. Hills
James Simpson and Chloroform   R. S. Atkinson
Edward Jenner and Vaccination   A. J. Harding Rains
Michael Faraday and Electricity   Brian Bowers
Louis Pasteur and Microbiology   H. I. Winner
Joseph Lister and Antisepsis   William Merrington
Rudolf Diesel and the Power Unit   John F. Moon

SBN 85078 128 0
Copyright © by Trevor I. Williams
First published in 1974 by
Priory Press Limited, 101 Grays Inn Road, London, W.C.1.
Text set in 12/14 pt. Monotype Baskerville, printed by photo-
lithography, and bound in Great Britain at The Pitman Press,
Bath

Contents

1 Nobel and his Prizes   9
2 The History of Explosives   13
3 Early Life   18
4 An International Business   29
5 Nobel and the Petroleum Industry   43
6 Nobel the Man   51
7 The Will and its Consequences   64
   Date Chart   87
   Glossary   90
   Further Reading   92
   Index   94
   Picture Credits   96

List of Illustrations

Portrait of Nobel	*frontispiece*
Boris Pasternak	8
Martin Luther King	8
Ernest Hemingway	8
Albert Einstein	10
Pierre and Marie Curie	11
The siege of Constantinople, 1453	12–13
Musketeer	14
The use of artillery at Marignano, 1515	14
"Brown Bess"	15
The Chassepot rifle	15
The destruction of Pot Rock, New York harbour	16
Olaf Rudbeck	18
Uppsala University	18
Immanuel Nobel Jr.	19
Andriette Nobel	19
Explosion of a Russian "Infernal Machine"	21
Alfred Nobel at the age of twenty	22
Stockholm	23
T. J. Pelouze	24
The *Monitor* vs. the *Merrimac*	25
John Ericcson	25
The factory at Winterwick	27
Early nitroglycerine manufacture—the one-legged stool	28–29
The Nobel factory at Ardeer, Scotland	30
Dynamite used for quarrying	32
Dynamite used for mining	33
Vieille's powder being tested	34–35
Sir Frederick Abel	36
The Nobel factory at Avigliana	36–37
San Remo, Italy	38
Dynamite factory in Switzerland	39

The Du Pont de Nemours factory, Delaware, U.S.A. 41
Nobel refinery at Baku 43
Rail transport for oil, Baku 44
Harbour at Baku 45
Oil steamer on the Caspian 46
Oil tanker *Rock Light* 47
S. A. Andrée's balloon attempt 48
Rolling gunpowder at the Bofors factory 49
Nobel's laboratory at the Bofors factory 50
Nobel's home near the Bofors factory 51
Nobel's writing desk 53
Nobel's writing desk 54
The Nobel House, Stockholm 55
Nobel's travelling bag 56
Percy Bysshe Shelley 59
Nobel in his laboratory at San Remo 60–61
Bertha von Suttner 62
Ragnar Sohlman 65
Nobel's will 66
Nobel Peace medal 68
The other Nobel Prize medals 69
The Nobel Library of the Swedish Academy 71
Carl Lindhagen 73
Nobel's House in Avenue Malakoff, Paris 74
The Nobel Institute for Physics and Chemistry 75
W. C. Röntgen 77
J. H. Van't Hoff 78
E. A. von Behring 79
R. F. A. Sully-Prudhomme 80
J. H. Dunant 81
F. Passy 82
Nobel's tomb 85

1 *Nobel and his Prizes*

The annual award of Nobel Prizes is an event of worldwide interest. Apart from their actual value—running into many thousands of pounds—these awards are the highest possible recognition of achievement in science and medicine, in literature, and in the cause of peace. Among the past prize-winners, some three hundred in all, are such famous people as Guglielmo Marconi, Albert Einstein, Marie Curie, Ernest Hemingway, Boris Pasternak, and Martin Luther King. Over the years, the prize-winners have come from almost every country in the world; they receive their awards from the King of Sweden at an impressive ceremony in Stockholm.

The awards are made each year on the same day, 10th December. The date is very significant, for it marks the anniversary of the death of an outstanding Swedish scientist, Alfred Nobel, whose remarkable industrial success made these prizes possible. Yet Nobel is less well known than many people who have received his prizes. There is a certain irony about this, for if the prizes had been founded by others in Nobel's lifetime, his own brilliance and success would probably have put him among the winners.

For this obscurity, Alfred Nobel himself was mainly responsible. Despite the scale of his world-wide industrial operations, he never courted publicity; indeed, he actively shunned it. To him, biography was of no interest. He did not trouble to put on record the sort of material that would help those who later sought to piece together the story of his life. Writing to his brother, he once said: "Who has time to read biographical accounts? And who can be so simple or so good-natured as to be in-

Famous Nobel Prize winners. *Top left* Boris Pasternak (1890–1960), the Russian Jewish novelist who won the Nobel Prize for Literature in 1958 after writing *Dr. Zhivago*. He was, however, heavily criticized in Russia and was forced to reject the award. *Top right* Martin Luther King (1929–68), the American minister and civil rights leader who won the peace prize in 1964. *Below* Ernest Hemingway (1899–1961), the American author and short story writer who won the Nobel Prize for Literature in 1954, seen here with his wife at a bullfight.

terested in them?" Pressed further, he said: "No one reads essays except about actors and murderers. . . ."

Perhaps Nobel's desire for anonymity should have been respected. He is for most people a rather shadowy person, known more for the prizes he endowed than for his own achievements. But he should be more widely recognized as an outstanding scientist and industrialist; and his life was extremely interesting and colourful.

From this point of view Nobel, as we shall see, was a man of baffling contradictions. Although he was immensely wealthy by the standards of his day, he lived relatively modestly and quietly. Generous to his guests, he was abstemious himself. Though his inventions greatly increased the destructiveness of military weapons, he was an ardent worker for the cause of peace. Though he received little formal education he mastered many aspects of science and engineering, and became fluent in the principal European languages: at nineteen he was writing verse in English that would have done credit to some of the minor poets. Despite poor health, he was amazingly energetic; few people ever achieved more than he did. A shrewd industrialist, he well knew the vital importance of precisely worded legal contracts; yet he drafted his own all-important will so imprecisely that years of litigation were necessary before his wishes could be fulfilled.

To use a Latin tag, Alfred Nobel was a man *sui generis*: that is, one who fits no ordinary category. Before trying to unravel this complex web we must, however, look at the main events in his life and the background against which they took place. As his main achievement was to build a vast international business to make high explosives, we must first learn something of the history of this industry up to the time that Nobel began to take an interest in it.

Albert Einstein (1879–1955), the German Jewish physicist, one of the greatest scientists since Isaac Newton. He won the Nobel Prize for Physics in 1921.

Marie and Pierre Curie jointly won the Nobel Prize for Physics in 1903 for the discovery of induced radioactivity. After Pierre's death in 1906, Marie Curie was also awarded the chemistry prize in 1911, one of the very few people ever to receive two prizes.

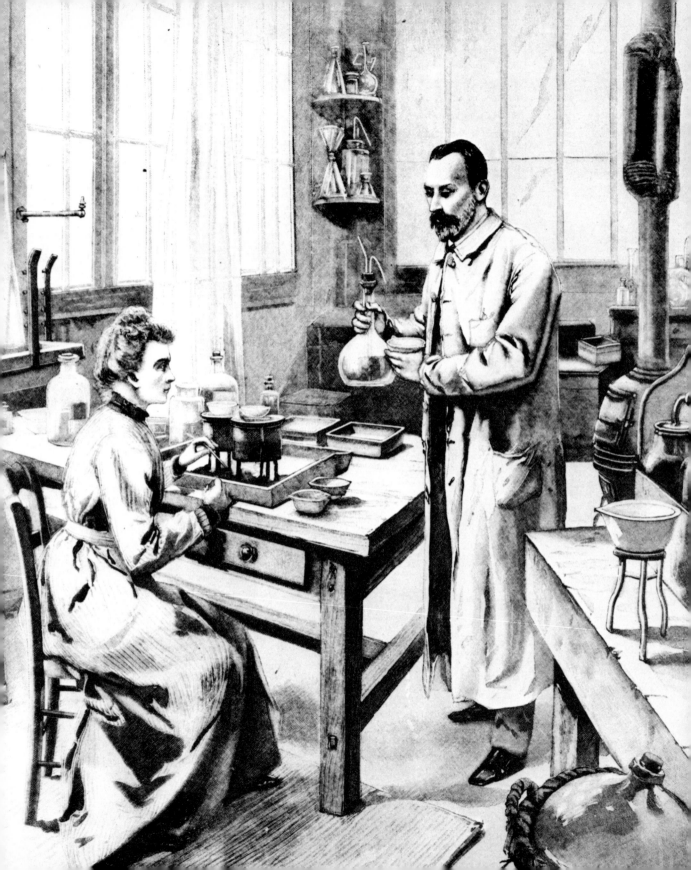

2 *The History of Explosives*

The details of the discovery of gunpowder are still obscure, but the main facts are well known. From ancient times—certainly as early as 500 B.C.—extensive military use was made of highly inflammable materials. The most famous of these was the so-called "Greek Fire" which, from the seventh century, played a big part in the defence of the Byzantine Empire. The exact composition of Greek Fire is doubtful, and probably no standard recipe existed, but the main ingredient was naphtha.

In about the eleventh century the Chinese found that such mixtures burned even more fiercely if saltpetre—which yields oxygen on heating—was added to them. From this it was quite a short step to gunpowder—described, but not invented, by Roger Bacon in the thirteenth century—a mixture of saltpetre, charcoal, and sulphur. This is "explosive" in the sense that once ignited it continues to burn even without air. A great quantity of hot gas is produced in a few seconds and the resulting high pressure can be used to bring about general destruction—for example, to destroy the foundations of a building—or controlled to fire projectiles from cannon or small arms such as muskets or pistols.

Artillery began to come into use in about the mid-thirteenth century, but Crécy (1346) was probably the first major European battle in which it was used. Guns were quite small at first, but as early as 1453

Greek Fire, here being used both offensively and defensively during the seige of Constantinople by the Turks in 1453.

13

the Turks used a nineteen-ton cannon in the siege of Constantinople. At first solid balls were fired, of stone or iron. But quite soon hollow projectiles were filled with gunpowder, and fused to explode on reaching their target. Sometimes such explosive shells were filled with small pieces of iron to rain a hail of small missiles on a massed enemy. Although explosive shells of this type were possibly used by the Venetians at Jadra in 1376, they were not widely used in warfare until the seventeenth century. Shrapnel, the invention of Henry Shrapnel (1761–1842), received official approval in 1803 and was extensively used in the Peninsular War and at Waterloo. The other important innovation in nineteenth-century artillery was that of the breech-loaded shell.

Meanwhile, hand firearms had begun to replace the long bow and the cross bow, which were old fashioned, though by no means extinct, by the seventeenth century. At first hand guns were

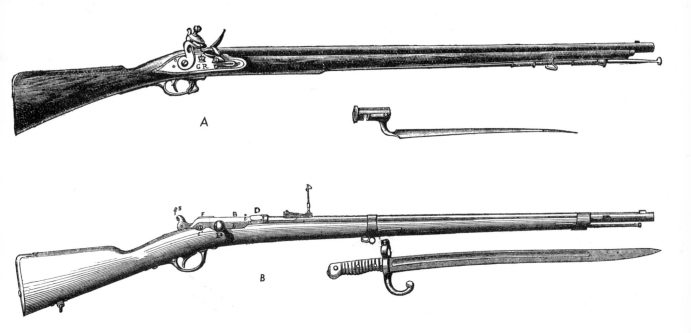

A

B

Opposite top Early musketeer with musket.
Above (a) "Brown Bess", officially known as the Long Land model, was one of the most famous models of musket. It was first used in the 1720s and had a 46-inch barrel and a wooden ramrod.
(b) The Chassepot rifle, an early French example of the breech-loading rifle, was first manufactured in 1870.

Left The use of artillery during the battle between Francis I of France and Swiss pikemen at Marignano in 1515.

clumsy inaccurate weapons, laboriously loaded by the muzzle and fired by applying a light to a touch-hole. But they evolved into accurate, reliable, quickfiring weapons. Spiral grooving of the barrel (rifling) gave a spin to the bullet, and greatly improved the accuracy. This device was known in the sixteenth century, for sporting purposes, but rifles did not come widely into military use until the Thirty Years' War (1618–48). The introduction of the percussion cap early in the nineteenth century provided a more reliable, weatherproof firing action. Finally, there was the introduction of the breech-loading cartridge, replacing the cumbersome method of muzzle-loading with a ramrod.

From the early days of gunpowder, military engineers had used it for undermining enemy fortifications, and from the 1600s it was used for blasting in mines and quarries. These were hazardous operations, but the risk was much reduced by William Bickford's invention of the safety fuse in 1831.

15

By the mid-nineteenth century the military and civil use of explosives was enormous; in 1851–53 some 100 tons were used in New York harbour alone to destroy Pot Rock. This last example deserves to be noted. High explosives are usually thought of as military weapons, but they also have immensely beneficial uses in mining, quarrying, and civil engineering. Surprisingly, gunpowder was still virtually the only explosive in use after five hundred years. The only significant change had been in how the ingredients were mixed. From early in the fifteenth century these were mixed wet instead of dry; apart from being safer, this "corned" powder was a more uniform and satisfactory material.

The use of massive charges of gunpowder to destroy Pot Rock in New York Harbour in 1851–53.

This, in brief, is the story of explosives up to the time of Alfred Nobel. In barely a quarter of a century he was to transform an industry which had hardly changed since mediaeval times. Meanwhile, however, the conditions for change were being established. In about 1845 C. F. Schönbein (1799–1868), Professor of Chemistry at Basle, found that if cotton and other forms of nearly pure cellulose are treated with nitric acid a highly explosive product (guncotton) is formed. Its explosive power was so much greater than that of gunpowder that in 1846 Schönbein patented it in Britain, and manufacture was started in a gunpowder works at Faversham, Kent. Guncotton factories were also built in France and elsewhere in Europe. In the summer of 1847 there was a disastrous explosion at Faversham and twenty-one men were killed. No further attempt at making guncotton was made in Britain at that time and in Europe the dangerous work was continued only in Austria. Many years elapsed before Sir Frederick Abel (1827–1902), of whom we shall hear more later, discovered how to make guncotton safe to handle.

At about the same time, another important discovery had been made in Italy. Ascanio Sobrero (1812–88), Professor of Chemistry at Turin, had found in 1846 that a violently explosive oily liquid (nitroglycerine) is produced by treating glycerine with nitric acid. This, too, proved far too unreliable to use. It was Alfred Nobel who transformed nitroglycerine from a dangerous chemical novelty into a safe and powerful explosive.

3 Early Life

How much is a man's life determined by inherited qualities, how much by environment and upbringing? These remain matters for heated argument. In Nobel's case both factors played a part. Although he came of quite humble parents, his great-great-great-grandfather was Olaf Rudbeck (1630–1702). Rudbeck was a gifted academic who became Rector of Uppsala University; keenly interested in science and medicine, he is said to have discovered the lymphatic system. He also published a major archaeological work entitled *Atlantica*. His name is used for the genus of plants known as Rudbeckia. Rudbeck's daughter Wendela married Petrus Oluffson, a law graduate of Uppsala University, who eventually became a judge. Their youngest son was Olaf Persson Nobelius (1706–60),

Above Olaf Rudbeck, Alfred Nobel's illustrious forebear who was Rector of Uppsala University in the seventeenth century.

Below Uppsala University shortly before Alfred Nobel's time.

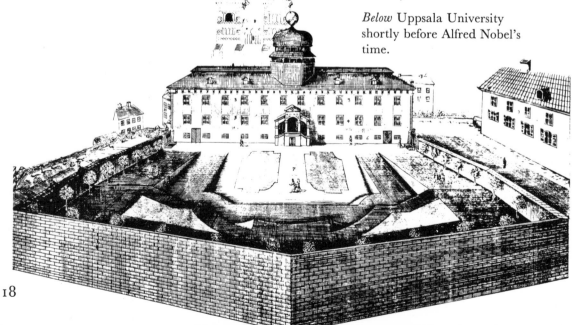

Above Immanuel Nobel Jr., Alfred Nobel's father.

Below Andriette Nobel, Alfred Nobel's mother.

a well-known miniature painter. Olaf's son, Alfred's grandfather, was Immanuel Nobelius (1757–1839). Immanuel was a doctor who changed his name to Nobel during his military service. Clearly, there was no lack of talent among Alfred Nobel's forebears on his father's side. Of his mother's family little is known, except that her name was Andriette Ahlsell and that she came from a south Swedish farming family. She was a devoted wife and mother, and Alfred was deeply attached to her.

Alfred's father was Immanuel Nobel (1801–72), a man who had certainly inherited his family's creative talents, but unfortunately had a notable lack of success in business. He was often away from home on speculative ventures. The family enjoyed an intellectually stimulating life, but their fortunes were erratic and at times they suffered severe poverty. They were often on the move and none of the children had much formal education; Alfred had no more than a couple of years (1841–42) at school in Stockholm. Nevertheless, later he became an honorary graduate of Uppsala University, where his illustrious ancestor Rudbeck had been Rector.

Immanuel Nobel's basic occupation is obscure. As a boy, he went to sea as a cabin boy, and on his return to Sweden began to study architecture. As a young man he seems to have survived mainly as a building contractor—with an unprofitable sideline as inventor. In 1833, one record describes him as an artist (though draughtsman is probably more correct), and he was apparently bankrupt: the year before the family home and all their possessions were destroyed by fire. Alfred was born in 1833, when his parents were in poor lodgings in Stockholm. He had two older brothers—Robert born in 1829, and Ludwig born in 1831—with whom, as we shall see, he was closely involved in various business enterprises. There were eight children, but only four survived to maturity. The youngest, Emil,

19

died in tragic circumstances when he was only twenty-one.

In 1837, partly to escape his creditors and partly to seek his fortune elsewhere, Immanuel left his family in Stockholm and went to Finland as an architect and builder. No doubt he sent home what money he could, but for five years the family's main support seems to have been a dairy and vegetable shop run by the mother. From Finland Immanuel went, in about 1840, to St. Petersburg (now Leningrad) in Russia, and set up as an engineer. For a time he prospered and in 1842, when Alfred was a boy of nine, he was able to send for his family to join him in Russia. Not only could the creditors be paid in full, but there was even money enough to hire private tutors for the boys. One of these was Nikolai Zinin (1811–80), a distinguished Professor of Chemistry.

The nature of Immanuel's work is important, for there is no doubt that it had a powerful effect on Alfred's career and on those of his brothers. While in Sweden Immanuel's inventive genius had turned to making mines for military use on land and at sea, but the Swedish government showed little interest. But in Russia things were different. Relations with the Western Powers were uneasy; Russia was looking to her armaments and the Ministry of War invited Immanuel to demonstrate his mines on land and at sea and paid him a fee for his work. It appears to have been this fee that enabled him to establish his factory.

Immanuel Nobel's mines were used at sea during the Crimean War, which broke out in 1854, but it seems they served more as a deterrent than a destructive weapon. His artistic talent is shown in a beautifully illustrated manuscript which describes an elaborate system of maritime defence using mines. The war brought a flood of orders from the Russian government for guns, large marine steam engines, ships' propellers, and other heavy engineering products. To meet these pressing demands, Immanuel expanded his factory with borrowed money, relying on the promise of the government—which in 1853 had awarded him a gold medal for services to Russian industry—that he could depend on plenty of orders. But Emperor Nicholas I died during the war, and when peace was signed the government abandoned Nobel and his factories and went back to placing most of its orders abroad. Once again Immanuel was ruined, and he returned to Sweden. He had, however, an unsuspected asset in

Explosion of a Russian "Infernal Machine"—or mine—on board *H.M.S. Exmouth.* It was devices such as these that Immanuel Nobel Jr. manufactured for the Russians during the Crimean War.

his three sons—Robert, Ludwig, and Alfred. The first two chose to remain in Russia, while Alfred gained valuable experience by travelling widely. The fourth son, Emil, who had been born in Russia, and was then only eighteen, returned with his parents to Stockholm.

As so often happens, the tide of fortune was turning just when things seemed at their worst. In St. Petersburg the two elder sons, Robert and Ludwig, applied themselves to salvaging what they could of the old business and embarking on new enterprises, including sawmills and a brickworks. In 1862 Robert, who had married a wealthy Finnish wife, left Russia to settle in Helsingfors. Shortly after-

Left Alfred Nobel at the age of twenty.

Below Stockholm as Alfred Nobel would have seen it as a youth.

ward, Ludwig embarked on an enterprise that was in the long run to be much more significant, the Aurora Lamp Oil Company. Initially, he was no more than a dealer but it gave him valuable experience of the petroleum industry, in which he and Alfred were later destined to play a very large role.

We have little information about Alfred's life during these years. His education with his tutors in St. Petersburg probably ended about 1850 when he was seventeen years old. The family fortune was then sufficient to send him on extensive travels to complete his education as an engineer. Alfred visited the main cities of Europe, observing and studying. He seems to have spent some time working in Paris in the laboratory of the distinguished chemist T. J. Pelouze (1807–67). He also spent some time, perhaps two years (probably 1850–2) in the United States. Here he met the brilliant Swedish engineer John Ericcson (1803–99), whose ironclad ship, the *Monitor*, played a decisive part in the Battle of Hampton Roads, in 1862. It is doubtful, however, whether Alfred actually worked with Ericcson.

Surviving correspondence reminds us that he achieved so much in spite of life-long ill-health. In the summer of 1854 he visited the health spa of Franzensbad to seek relief. He had to drive himself relentlessly, all the time.

Eventually he went back to St. Petersburg to join his brothers in the business there, and the experience gained through his travels made him a valuable asset. Not only had he had good training in engineering and chemistry, but he had studied foreign business methods. In addition he had a good command of German, English, French, and Russian.

For the moment, however, we must return to Immanuel Nobel, for the story of Alfred's early life is very much the story of the Nobel family.

Above T. J. Pelouze (1807–67), French chemist who discovered nitrocellulose.

Top right The *Monitor* vs. the *Merrimac* in the Battle of Hampton Roads, March 1862, during the Civil War in America. The building of these "ironclads" marked a turning point in the history of naval warfare.

Right John Ericcson (1803–1899), the Swedish American mechanical engineer, whose many achievements included the design of the warship *Monitor*.

When Immanuel returned to Stockholm after the collapse of his Russian business he was sixty. He courageously set about building a new business and in 1863 was busy manufacturing a form of gunpowder which used sodium chlorate instead of the traditional nitrate. Optimistic as always, he visualized great sales for this abroad, especially in Russia. He wrote to Alfred in St. Petersburg, urging him to return to Stockholm to help him. This letter came at a good moment, for Alfred had himself developed a keen interest in explosives, trying to find a safe way of using Sobrero's nitroglycerine. He had learned something about this from his old tutor in St. Petersburg, Professor Zinin, and doubtless also from Pelouze in Paris. Also, much information about its manufacture and use had been published in the scientific journals, for all to read, by Sobrero, Pelouze, and others. When his father's letter arrived, Alfred had already prepared nitroglycerine and had successfully exploded small charges under water. But his visit to Stockholm was a disappointment, for the new gunpowder failed to live up to its promise.

It turned out that Immanuel, too, had been experimenting with nitroglycerine and had tried to make it safer and more manageable by mixing it with gunpowder to produce a sort of dough. Although the mixture was more powerful than gunpowder it fell far short of the explosive potential of the nitroglycerine contained in it.

Alfred had also been looking at the possibility of combining gunpowder and nitroglycerine, but in a quite different way. Nitroglycerine is a treacherous substance. Although very inflammable, its burning does not always lead to an explosion; it may just burn away with a bright flame, like alcohol. It is only when the combustion gets out of hand, as it were, that the dramatically explosive properties reveal themselves. For practical use, this variability is a grave disadvantage. Apart from wanting an explosion of predictable force every time, the civil or military engineer never wants to have left on his hands a quantity of unexploded material which is unsafe to handle. Alfred realized that while sudden heat might detonate nitroglycerine, this could be done more reliably by a sharp shock whose waves would permeate the whole of the material. To obtain this shock, he used gunpowder, itself exploded by a detonator. Although apparently simple, this was a decisive invention and it paved the way to the successful exploitation of nitroglycerine, which Nobel regarded as his greatest achievement.

This success was not immediate, however. At first, the new discovery started a quarrel between father and son. Immanuel, not realizing that this use of gunpowder was in principle quite different from his own, accused his son of claiming his discovery as his own. In a polite, but very sharp, letter Alfred defended his position and his father recognized that the credit for the discovery, and the valuable patent relating to it, was Alfred's alone.

Some time in the latter part of 1863, father and son set up a small works at Heleneborg, near their home in Stockholm, for making nitroglycerine. Alfred's youngest brother, Emil—still only twenty years old—was also employed in the works. For a year all went well and small quantities of nitroglycerine were sold for quarrying, mining, and railway construction. Then, on 3rd September, 1864, there was a violent explosion: Emil and four workmen were killed. The precise cause was never known, but it is possible that Emil, with the best of motives, had departed from the prescribed process of manufacture.

The disaster was, of course, a grievous loss to the Nobel family, and soon afterwards Immanuel suffered a severe stroke. He lived until 1872, and recovered his mental faculties, but his remaining years were those of an invalid. In these tragic circumstances, the whole burden of the nascent Swedish nitroglycerine industry fell on Alfred. The problems before him were considerable. The Helene-

The explosives factory at Winterwick, near Stockholm.

borg disaster aroused great public indignation and he was hard put to it to justify carrying out such a dangerous procedure in a populous area. For a long time he could find no other site within the city area, even though there was still a pressing demand for the product, especially needed to complete the last stage of the state railway into Stockholm. Eventually an acceptable solution was found by manufacturing on a barge anchored in Malar Lake, near Stockholm.

Production was still on a small scale for local use, and was in the hands of the Nitro-Glycerine Company founded by Alfred and Immanuel Nobel, in collaboration with others. Not until March 1865 was the world's first real high explosives factory established, at Winterwick, near Stockholm. The manufacturing process was very simple. It really amounted to no more than a scaled-up version of Sobrero's laboratory process. The use of pumps and other machinery was deliberately avoided, to eliminate the possibility of excessive local heating through friction or other causes and the accumulation of pockets of dangerous material. The plant was arranged so that the liquid reagents and products flowed under gravity.

At this time, more than a century ago, many people had little understanding of the nature of nitroglycerine. Often it was treated in an appallingly casual way. It was generally transported to the point where it was used in small cans or bottles packed in wooden crates. If some were broken or leaked on the way, no one worried. On one occasion, oil that had leaked was used to lubricate a cart, and on another to dress the leather of a harness. However, luck did not always favour the ignorant or foolhardy. As we shall see later, the early manufacture and use of the new explosive caused so many fatal accidents that the very existence of the new industry was threatened.

A stage in the manufacture of nitroglycerine by the early batch method. The processman sits on a one-legged stool, a device to ensure that he would be wakened should he nod off as he watched the thermometer during a critical stage of process.

4 *An International Business*

Up to the founding of the Winterwick factory in 1865, Alfred Nobel's nitroglycerine operations had been entirely Swedish. He soon decided that the business must be developed internationally, and during the next decade factories were established throughout Europe and in North America. Production near the site where it was used had obvious economic advantages, particularly with a material needing such careful handling. Nevertheless, from the early days quite a big export business was built up by many of the factories.

Nobel's first factory outside Sweden was built at Krümmel, on the River Elbe near Hamburg, in 1865. By 1873 he had also opened works in Norway, Finland, Bohemia, Scotland, France, Spain, Switzerland, Italy, Portugal and Hungary. In 1868 came the first big American venture, the Giant Powder Company in San Francisco. However, these ventures were fraught with danger and the advice of Alfred Nobel, as the expert on nitroglycerine, was sought all the time.

A series of accidents bedevilled the whole industry. The worst occurred in 1866, when the steamship *European* blew up with the loss of seventy-four lives. Almost simultaneously fourteen lives were lost in an explosion in a warehouse in San Francisco. In the same year, the Krümmel factory was destroyed and there was a big explosion in Sydney, Australia. Public feeling ran high and many countries either banned the manufacture of nitroglycerine altogether or restricted its transport and use so severely as to have virtually the same effect.

Despite all his business cares, and almost constant travel, Alfred Nobel gave much attention to making nitroglycerine safe to use without weakening

Dynamite Mixing

Scott, Pho
Ardross

its explosive force. At first, he pinned his hopes to the device of adding methyl alcohol to the manufactured product; this much reduced its readiness to explode and could easily be washed out with water immediately before use. It was, however, a troublesome arrangement and he experimented with mixing nitroglycerine with some inert material that would give a solid product.

He may well have been influenced by his father's early experiments in mixing nitroglycerine with gunpowder, and by knowing that nitroglycerine leaking from containers sometimes formed a paste with the powder in which they were packed. But there is no doubt that Nobel's new invention arose, not from chance, but from thinking about the basic principles involved. After trying all kinds of absorbents—including charcoal, cement, and brickdust—he finally found the ideal in a common form of clay known as *kieselguhr*, which is particularly porous. He patented the use of this in 1867 and from then on began to manufacture dynamite, as the mixture of *kieselguhr* and nitroglycerine was called. Despite the clear advantages of the new product, it was some thirty years before the more conservative mining companies, especially in Sweden, finally stopped asking for liquid nitroglycerine.

The new dynamite profoundly changed the fortunes of the troubled nitroglycerine industry. Production rose rapidly and in five years multiplied several hundred times. When Nobel addressed the Society of Arts in London in 1875, he told his audience that the sale of dynamite in the previous year had exceeded 3,000 tons. This compared with 424 tons in 1870 and only 11 tons in 1867. These figures, which appeared very impressive then, are of course far lower than today's sales.

Dynamite was a great improvement, but it still was not quite satisfactory. The dilution with inert *kieselguhr* diminished the explosive force of the nitro-

Left above The Nobel factory at Ardeer, Scotland in 1897. This photograph shows hand-mixing of the original "Red Dynamite."

Left below The Ardeer factory. Before entering the danger zone, the girls were searched to make sure that they were not carrying metallic objects—which might give rise to sparks—such as hair pins, safety pins or metal buttons.

31

glycerine. Also, the product was liable to "sweat" and exude dangerous drops of liquid nitroglycerine. In the end, Nobel found a way of mixing nitroglycerine with guncotton or nitrocellulose. The secret of his success lay in using cotton (or some other form of cellulose) which was less highly nitrated than usual. His product—"blasting gelatine"—was perfected in 1875. Its explosive properties and consistency could be varied by varying

Dynamite being used for quarrying.

Dynamite being used for mining.

the proportions of the two ingredients; generally the nitrocellulose content lay between 2.5 and 7 per cent.

All these types of explosives were primarily suited for general rock blasting, and in this field the supremacy of gunpowder was quickly destroyed. Dynamite, for example, is about five times more powerful than gunpowder. For other purposes, especially military purposes, gunpowder was much less easily replaced. Alfred Nobel explained why in his lecture to the Society of Arts, already mentioned in, 1875: "It is difficult, even with more powerful explosives at command, to supersede gunpowder. That old mixture possesses a truly admirable elasticity which permits its adaptation to purposes of the most varied nature. Thus, in a mine, it is wanted to blast without propelling; in a gun to propel without blasting; in a shell it serves both purposes combined; in a fuse, as in fireworks, it burns quite slowly without exploding. Its pressure, exercised in these numerous operations, varies between one ounce (more or less) to the square inch, in a fuse and 85,000 lbs to the square inch in a shell."

For military purposes a smokeless explosive was wanted. It would not give away the position of artillery in action, and would cause less fouling of the gun barrel. Several inventors applied themselves to this. The first to achieve success was Major J. F. E. Schultze (1825–74) of the Prussian Artillery, who in about 1865 introduced a powder based on nitrated wood mixed with saltpetre. This was suitable for artillery and shotguns, but too violent for rifles. Schultze powder was manufactured in England from 1868.

Another kind of smokeless powder was invented in 1882 by W. F. Reid and D. Johnson, at the Explosives Company at Stowmarket, England. In granular form, it was based on nitrocotton mixed

33

with saltpetre and partially gelatinized with a mixture of alcohol and ether. Again, it was too powerful for rifles. In France, P. M. E. Vieille (1854–1934) developed an explosive based on fully gelatinized nitrocotton. The dough-like material was rolled into thin sheets, diced, and dried. It was known as Poudre B (a tribute to General E. J. M. Boulanger (1837–91), at that time in command of the army of occupation in Tunis).

Alfred Nobel now made his contribution, with the introduction of ballistite in 1888. The development was both new and surprising. Nobel had found that if nitrocotton and nitroglycerine are mixed, each violent partner seems to tame the other. The mixture does not explode so much as burn ferociously, but with great regularity. It therefore makes a good propellant. Experience showed

Vieille's powder being tested. *Below* Ordinary powder being used. *Opposite* Vieille's smokeless powder being similarly used.

that some other ingredients, such as camphor, improved the explosive characteristics.

Yet ballistite was to cause Nobel much disappointment. In 1869, the British government had passed an Act of Parliament virtually banning the use of nitroglycerine, or preparations containing it, such as dynamite. Nobel regarded this as discrimination and largely put it down to prejudice on the part of Sir Frederick Abel (1827–1902), the British government's chief adviser on explosives, in favour of guncotton. Abel had made the major discovery that guncotton could be stabilized by extremely thorough washing to remove every trace of acid. Eventually the quarrel was made up and Nobel and Abel became good friends. Unfortunately, the discovery of ballistite was to revive the quarrel.

Right The dynamite factory at Avigliana.

Left Sir Frederick Abel (1827–1902).

In 1888, the British government set up an Explosives Commission to advise it on the best use of the new discoveries in this field, especially in the military context. Abel was a member of this Commission, and in close touch with Nobel, who was very frank with him. The Commission expressed doubts about ballistite, mainly because the camphor in it was volatile and so would gradually disappear. Nobel suggested various ways of eliminating this defect.

Meanwhile, however, Abel, together with another distinguished chemist Sir James Dewar (1842–1923), had developed and patented a modification containing a little acetone and petroleum jelly. This was named cordite: it was plastic enough to be extruded through a die in the form of cord, which could then be chopped into pellets. Abel and Dewar made over their English patent rights to the British government, but retained—and exercised—the rights of exploitation abroad. Understandably,

Nobel regarded this as an infringement of his own patent and protested strongly. Since he received no satisfaction, it was agreed to institute "friendly" proceedings so that the case could be argued formally in the British courts. The case lasted two years (1893–95), going to the Court of Appeal and then to the House of Lords. The verdict finally went against Nobel, mainly because of an alleged looseness of expression in the drafting of his own patent. The suit cost Nobel £28,000 and left him very embittered.

Elsewhere, too, ballistite landed Nobel in serious trouble. The first government to take it up was the Italian, who in 1889 placed an initial contract for some 300 tons with its Avigliana factory; Nobel was to receive a royalty. Soon afterwards, the Italian government concluded an exclusive royalty agreement with Nobel. This caused a strong reaction in France, where Nobel was then living, because the French government was strongly backing Vieille's smokeless powder, to which Nobel's product was a serious rival. As a result of this, Nobel's laboratory in Paris was shut down; his factory at Honfleur had to suspend its operations; and he was denied vital testing facilities. In 1891 Nobel, disillusioned, left France and went to live, for the five remaining years of his life, in Italy, mainly in San Remo.

In one way and another, these were all years of prodigious activity. Apart from spending much time in the laboratory making and developing his inventions, Nobel had quickly built up a complex international manufacturing and marketing organization. He had his own factories in the major countries of the world; he made reciprocal manufacturing arrangements with other companies, and

Above right Packing cartridges into boxes, and *below* filling cartridges with powder at a munitions factory in Switzerland in 1893.

Below San Remo, Italy, where Nobel spent the last five years of his life.

appointed agents in other countries. Although part of one industrial empire, each company had a life and loyalty of its own and clashes of interest were by no means uncommon. Another cause of trouble was that involvement in politics was unavoidable because of the nature of the business. As the man with his finger on the pulse of the whole concern, as well as being the technical expert, Nobel was constantly in demand to resolve problems. This intervention was inescapable, but against his better judgement. In a letter to his brother Robert in 1883 he wrote: "We must confine ourselves to the work of thinking, and leave all the mechanics to others."

Eventually most of the business was arranged in two large trust companies. One, the Nobel Dynamite Trust Company, in London, concerned itself mainly with the British and German interests. The other, the Société Centrale de Dynamite, in Paris, looked after the French, Swiss, Italian, South American, and certain other interests. As the enterprise grew, so did the number of associates on whom Nobel was dependent, and he was not always fortunate in his choice. Indeed, one of them, Paul Barbe, seemed at one time to have ruined him utterly. Paul Barbe and his father were ironfounders near Nancy and in 1868 Nobel signed an agreement with them to market his explosive products in France. Barbe was exceptionally gifted and industrious, and for many years the partnership worked well. Unfortunately, Barbe was also unscrupulous and politically very ambitious. Nobel knew this, but believed that the weakness could be contained and was far out-weighed by Barbe's exceptional ability.

In 1883, he wrote to his brother Robert about Barbe, saying: "He has a marvellous scientific imagination, is an exceptionally good salesman, a far-seeing business man, and knows how to make the best of people and to get out of each man the in-

The Du Pont de Nemours & Co.'s Upper Brandywine Gunpowder Mills, near Wilmington, Delaware, U.S.A. about 1880.

dividual work of which he is capable. His own achievements are as incredible as his power to work; but he is unreliable unless his personal interest is involved. This is a hateful defect. . . ." Barbe realized his political ambition—which was, of course, very helpful to Nobel in his dealings with the French government—and at the time of his death in 1890 had for some years been Minister of Agriculture. After his death, however, it was found that Barbe had been implicated in the notorious Panama Scandal and some of his associates in the Société Centrale de Dynamite had speculated unsuccessfully in glycerine using the company's

41

money. For a time, Nobel contemplated the necessity of becoming an employee in his own business in Germany, because of these financial difficulties, but in the end his resources, and resourcefulness, were enough to save the situation.

In the United States, too, his experience was not happy. There one of his associates, T. P. Shaffner, proved treacherous and tried to rob Nobel of his patent rights in the use of nitroglycerine. Long and costly litigation was needed to restore the situation. The booming development in America greatly increased the demand for explosives, but there was strong opposition from established gunpowder manufacturers, especially the powerful firm of Du Pont de Nemours at Wilmington. Generally speaking the business was more troublesome than profitable, and Nobel withdrew from his American interests altogether in 1885.

For a man in robust health, the constant travel, meetings, and anxieties connected with the rapid establishment of a large worldwide enterprise, would have been exhausting enough. That a man whose health had been frail from childhood should have done so much is remarkable. Yet more remarkable is the fact that, in addition, he not only managed some very large enterprises of a quite different kind, but was also an active worker in the cause of international peace. These other facets of the character of this exceptional man we must now consider.

5 *Nobel and the Petroleum Industry*

Alfred's older brother Ludwig stayed behind in St. Petersburg after their father went back to Stockholm. Ludwig applied himself to making a living as an engineer. At first he worked for the creditors as a salaried employee of the old family business, responsible for winding it up. Before long, however, he was back in business on his own account as a manufacturing engineer. Ludwig began to make artillery and other firearms, and converted muzzle-loading muskets into breech-loaders. In this business he was rejoined by his brother Robert in 1870. Later he worked on a major contract to provide 450,000 rifles for the Russian government. Surprisingly, it was this that led the brothers into the oil business.

Traditionally, good rifle butts are made of walnut, and Robert went to the Caucasus to see whether he could buy the wood there. Some wood was obtained, though not enough. But on this trip Robert saw for himself how petroleum was

The oil fields of the Nobel refinery at Baku, 1882.

Oil being transported by rail to Baku in the 1880s.

being extracted and processed at Baku on the Caspian Sea. Though still very primitive, the petroleum industry was an old one, and had been described by Marco Polo, who visited Baku in 1272. Russia had acquired the oil-producing regions from Persia in 1806.

When he got back to St. Petersburg, Robert persuaded Ludwig to help him set up a Caspian oil business. The enterprise was a great success. Des-

44

pite the rough terrain, their lack of knowledge of the business, and the hostility of other operators, the business grew with remarkable speed. The brothers introduced all kinds of new techniques: oil pipelines, tanker ships for conveying the oil by sea or river, rail tank-cars to transport it by land. More remarkable, for the times, was their attitude towards their workers. Near their works they built a "garden city", with houses for the workers set in parkland with a range of libraries, billiard halls,

The harbour at Baku.

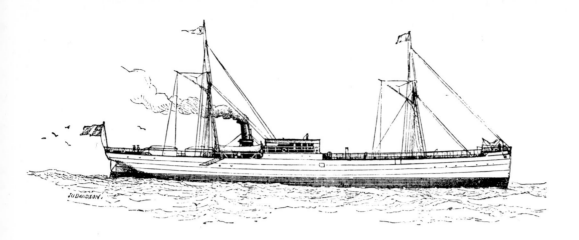

and other public buildings for recreation, and schools for the children. Recognizing that the success of any business depends on the loyalty and enthusiasm of its workers, the brothers started a workers' profit-sharing scheme, almost unheard of in those days. To encourage thrift, a savings bank was established.

Yet there were great difficulties, especially in raising the necessary finance. It was in this connection that Alfred once again became closely involved with his two elder brothers. As early as 1875 Ludwig had written to Alfred hoping to persuade him to visit Baku, but for a long time Alfred preferred to watch the development of the business at a distance. In 1877 the two brothers met in Paris, and in the following year agreed to form the Nobel Brothers' Naphtha Company; the articles of association were formally approved by the Emperor of Russia in the following year.

At first, Alfred's holding was a modest ten per cent, but this increased over the years as the company raised new capital to finance its phenomenally rapid expansion. In 1883 he became for a short time a director, mainly to curb what he regarded as over-spending. By 1898 the company had grown so fast that it had a fleet of no less than fifty-three tankers, capable of carrying 80,000 tons of oil.

The tankers had been built in Sweden and brought through an elaborate system of inland waterways from the Baltic Sea to the Caspian Sea: the largest had to be built in two parts in order to negotiate the locks. Vast storage tanks had to be built, partly because of the seasonal nature of the business. At that time, before the advent of the motor car, the main outlet was as lamp oil, and naturally the demand for this was greatest during the dark winter months. On the technical side Ludwig showed the same flair and compulsive urge to work as Alfred did on the financial side.

Although explosives and petroleum were Alfred Nobel's main industrial interests, his restless mind turned itself in many other directions and in the course of his lifetime he took out more than 350 patents. These ranged over such diverse fields as artificial fibres, synthetic rubber, paints (based on nitrocellulose), sound reproduction and artificial gems. Late in life, in 1895, he founded an electro-chemical works in Sweden with the engineer Rudolf Lilljeqvist, who was to be one of the executors of his will. He had interests in the manufacture of bicycles, boilers, and turbines. At one time he became inter-

The 5,000 ton *Rock Light* oil tanker built in 1899.

ested in blood transfusion. He even helped to finance
S. A. Andrée's ill-fated attempt to reach the North
Pole in a balloon in 1897. He clearly foresaw, however, that the future of aviation lay not in balloons
but in mechanically propelled aircraft: "We must
not think of solving this problem by means of
balloons. . . . We have to have floating rafts driven
forward at great speed."

S. A. Andrée and his ill-fated
balloon.

In 1894, in spite of increasingly frequent heart attacks, Nobel set off on yet another journey. He first visited London, where an appeal to the House of Lords was being prepared in the cordite case, and then went on to Sweden. His object was to establish a works in Sweden suitable for the manufacture of modern armaments, and in pursuit of this he visited the Bofors-Gullspräng Company, owners of a steelworks at Bofors, in which he had a majority shareholding. Bofors suited his needs very well, and it was here that many of the speculative experi-

Rolling gunpowder at the Bofors works.

ments mentioned above were carried out. Close by, at Björkborn, he bought a fine country house as a residence in the summer months, wintering in San Remo in Italy. The remote location suited him in many ways; it was away from the turmoil of Paris, where he had been so harassed, and from the irritation of San Remo where his neighbours had objected to his noisy ballistic experiments. It also gave him once again a footing in his native country, to which in his later years his sympathies were increasingly turning after long years of travel and self-imposed exile. He once called himself the richest vagabond in Europe.

Nobel's laboratory at the Bofors factory.

6 Nobel the Man

Björkborn, Värmland, Nobel's Swedish home, near the Bofors factory.

What was Alfred Nobel like as a person? This is already implied in the things he did: thus we are already conscious of a man with a powerful and wide-ranging intellect, a flair for finance, a huge capacity for work, determination in the face of difficulties, and a strong sense of family unity. Much more than this can, however, be inferred from other evidence, for we know something of

Nobel's estimation of himself and others have left on record their views of him. Neither type of evidence, of course, is to be too heavily relied upon, for there is always the danger of self-deception or prejudice. Yet he was such a mass of contradictions that no simple interpretation of his personality is convincing. However, one thread that certainly runs through his life is that of loneliness, and this explains many of the things he did. His loneliness was not that of the recluse for he was always in contact with a large number of people. Rather was it the loneliness that comes from inability to form close human relationships, and reluctance to delegate. He had a wide circle of acquaintances but few friends. He once referred to "chance acquaintances, with whom one can, of course, spend a few pleasant hours, but from whom one later parts with as much regret as from an old worn-out coat."

Although by no means indifferent to women, he never married. In 1887 he wrote: "For the past nine days I have been ill and have had to stay indoors with no other company than a paid valet. . . . When at the age of fifty-four one is left so alone in the world, and a paid servant is the only person who has so far showed one the most kindness, then come heavy thoughts, heavier than most people can imagine." He lived alone, and he died alone.

Possibly one cause of his loneliness was his chronic ill health, which even in childhood cut him off from many everyday activities. From about 1889 his heart trouble became serious. It probably made him even more self-sufficient. He also had the Swedish tendency to melancholy. Certainly he was given at times to self-pity. Thus in a letter to his sister-in-law he contrasts her happy family life with his own loneliness: "I, drifting about with no compass or helm like a useless wreck battered by fate, without bright memories from the past, without the false but beautiful light of illusion for the future. . . ."

Nobel's writing desk, preserved in the Nobel Rooms of the Nobel Library of the Swedish Academy.

Nobel's writing desk, with various small personal belongings.

A detached look at Nobel's life does not really engender much sympathy for this sort of pleading, for so far as it was true, it was of his own making. Although he was punctilious in his family relationships, remembering anniversaries by writing and gifts, even this seems—except in the case of his mother, to whom he was devoted—to have been somewhat impersonal. When he was aroused, his temper could be fierce but it quickly subsided. His wealth permitted him to live where and as he pleased. His home, wherever it might be, was well appointed and well served. He never smoked or drank himself, but his guests were always well looked after in these respects. In his dress he was unostentatious but always neat and appropriate.

The Nobel House, Stockholm, seat of the Nobel Foundation.

Although a celebrity in his own time, Nobel was invariably modest and given to self-depreciation; his instinct was always to remain in the background. He hated purely social gatherings and so far as he could, without giving offence, declined all public honours. Sarcastically, he once said that he owed his Swedish Order of the North Star to his cook, who had once pleased an influential stomach. He never sat for his portrait. Once, when he was asked for a picture to appear in some anniversary publication of one of his works, he refused unless every single workman was asked to do the same: "Then I will send a reproduction of my pig's-bristle bachelor snout, not before."

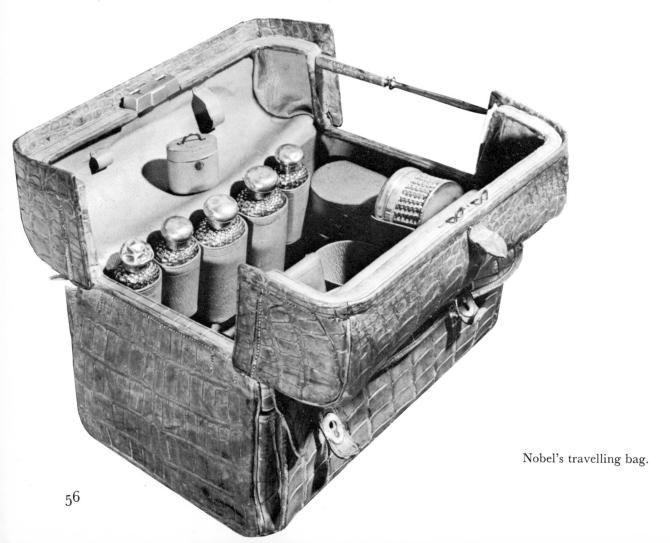

Nobel's travelling bag.

He had to keep in touch with political events, because he had constantly to engage in negotiations with strong political overtones, but he never hid his contempt for politics as such. He regarded them as mainly a platform for intrigue and self-advancement. Perhaps this modesty was to some extent deliberately assumed, but of its practical consequences there is no doubt. With Swedish realism, Nobel knew the importance of social life, even though it gave him little personal pleasure. He once wrote: "He who withdraws himself from all cultured society, and neglects to keep alive the interchange of ideas with thoughtful persons, finally loses the capacity to do so. . . ."

We have seen that ordinary relaxation found little place in Alfred Nobel's life. He had no interest in music but he did find solace in literature both as a reader and, more particularly, as a writer. In his reading, he preferred idealistic and imaginative, to descriptive, writers. He had, of course, to do a tremendous amount of writing in his business, but apart from this he had to his credit a number of purely literary compositions which are not without merit. The earliest, a poem in English of 425 lines, is of interest for the biographical information it provides on his early years, and the light it throws on his attitude to life. Considering that he was only eighteen when he wrote it, and his native language was Swedish, it is a very remarkable achievement.

> *"This breathing clay, what business has it here?*
> *Some petty wants to chain us to the earth.*
> *Some lofty thoughts to lift us to the spheres*
> *And cheat us with that semblance of a soul,*
> *To dream of immortality . . ."*

This command of poetic English is in striking contrast with his poor showing with Swedish prose. An unfinished novel, *Brothers and Sisters* which he probably wrote when he was about thirty, is almost totally lacking in merit. Certainly he was most successful with poetry, and perhaps this reflects the inventive genius of his mind which was the basis of his success in business. It would seem that he often turned to writing as some sort of solace in a period of ill health or business anxiety. Thus the outcome of the great cordite case in England (pages 36–7) inspired a bitingly sarcastic comedy, never completed, called *The Patent Bacillus*.

In his poetry Nobel was much influenced by Shelley, and at the end of his life he set himself to write in Swedish a tragedy in four acts entitled *Nemesis*. Its theme, like Shelley's *The Cenci* (1819) is the life of the depraved fifteenth-century Roman nobleman, Francesco Cenci, who treated his four sons with abominable cruelty and debauched his daughter Beatrice. In Nobel's version the incestuous relationship with Beatrice is eliminated by making it appear that Cenci was not her father. The play was on the point of publication at the time of Nobel's death, and was suppressed by his family on the ground that it would do him no credit. By the standards of nearly a century ago it would have been regarded as outspoken and Nobel himself was worried about the attitude of the Swedish censor. Today, however, it would be regarded as quite harmless. It would seem, from the three copies that survived, that publication would certainly have done him no harm.

Alfred Nobel was not a man of deep religious conviction, but he certainly subscribed to the basic Christian principles. A Lutheran by upbringing, he actively supported the Swedish Church in Paris while he lived there. To its pastor, Nathan Söderblom—later Archbishop of Sweden—he once wrote: "The difference in our religious views is perhaps formal rather than real, for we both agree that we should do to our neighbour what we want him to do to us." Characteristically, he could not refrain from going on to make a dig at himself: "Admittedly

I go a step further, for I have a loathing for myself which I by no means have for my neighbour." Inevitably, he was the recipient of a large number of begging letters, many from women. He once said that these averaged more than a hundred a week, with demands for more than ten thousand pounds. Most deservedly received a trenchant reply, but there were many who had cause to remember his generosity, which was always unobtrusively expressed.

In his later years Nobel took an active part in the cause of world peace through his encouragement of various peace movements. But he had been interested in this cause for a long time. To some extent, no doubt, this was stimulated by his long-standing admiration for Shelley, who had strong pacifist views. To some, Nobel's championship of peace savours of hypocrisy, symptomatic of a bad

Right Percy Bysshe Shelley, the poet, from whom Nobel drew much inspiration.

conscience in a man who had made such terrible weapons of destruction. As plausibly, and more charitably, it may be seen as another aspect of his difficulty over personal relationships; while individual men (and women) were a problem to him, he could be enthusiastic about mankind as a whole and about peace as an abstract idea.

Nobel was in touch with many of the pacifist leaders of his time, and much has been made of his relationship with Bertha von Suttner, the Austrian writer and worker for peace, to whom we will return later. He had no patience with impractical ideals. "What we need," he wrote in 1891, "is not money but a programme." His own programme was essentially one of political agreement between the great powers. All would unite against one that broke the peace. By such a means a prolonged period of peace might be assured and then, and only then, a progressive disarmament programme might be politically feasible. Meanwhile, armaments might serve better to preserve peace than "resolutions, banquets, and long speeches." Prophetically, he looked forward to "the day when two army corps will be able to destroy each other in one second [and] all civilized nations will recoil from war in horror and disband their armies." With the atom bomb, this fearful threat has become reality; how far it has contributed to the avoidance of another world war during the past thirty years must be a matter of opinion.

The Peace Congress at Berne in 1892 seems to have been something of a turning-point in Nobel's ideas. Although he attended only briefly, it was long enough for him to form an incisive opinion. He wrote: "I was astonished no less by the rapidly increasing number of able and serious members than by the ridiculous efforts made by gasbags, which must spoil the best cause. To demand disarmament or unconditional arbitration is, in the present state

60

Alfred Nobel in his laboratory at San Remo, Italy; from the painting by Professor Österman.

of mind of the persons in power, to incur the responsibility of putting forward ridiculous proposals which cannot be of the slightest use to anyone." As his own contribution, he determined in 1893 to leave part of his fortune to award a prize periodically "to the man or woman who had done most to advance the idea of general peace in Europe." We shall see later how he carried out this intention.

No account of Nobel's life would be complete without some mention of the part women played in it. Here, he had none of the success that marked his business ventures, or the story of his life might have been very different. Apart from his mother, for whom he had a deep and lasting affection until her death in 1889, only seven years before his own, there were three women who were important in his life. The first we cannot identify, but she is explicitly mentioned in the biographical poem from which we have already quoted. As this was probably written about 1851 it is likely that it was a girl he met as a young student in Paris. Tragically, she died as their love blossomed:

> *"This might have ended in the usual manner*
> *And brought the joys and griefs of wedded life;*
> *But 'twas not so ordained; another bridegroom*
> *Had stronger claims—she's wedded to her grave."*

He reproaches himself bitterly that he was not with her when she died:

> *". . . My love is with the dead.*
> *Nor was I there to soothe her latest hour,*
> *But came to gaze upon a putrid corpse,*
> *Such as but fools can cherish."*

In 1876, when he was forty-three, Nobel—describing himself as "an elderly gentleman"—advertised for a private secretary. Among those who replied was an attractive young woman, the Countess Bertha Kinsky, daughter of an impoverished Austrian family. After an exchange of letters they met in Paris, and she was given the job.

61

It seems, however, that Nobel was not as old as he had supposed, and he seems immediately to have lost his heart to the Countess. Unfortunately for him her affections were already bestowed. She very soon left him, to make a runaway marriage with the young Austrian novelist Baron Arthur Gundaccar von Suttner, to whom she was already secretly engaged in defiance of her family's wishes. As Bertha von Suttner she became well known as an ardent worker for peace, and on this subject Nobel carried on a long, and entirely platonic, correspondence with her. It seems, however, that after she left her job as secretary, they actually met only twice, the first time not until more than ten years had passed, and the second when she and her husband stayed with Nobel for a few days in Switzerland.

Later that year Nobel was in Austria and made his way to the health resort of Baden-bei-Wien. There, making a casual purchase in a flower shop, he made the acquaintance of an unsophisticated young Jewish girl, Sophie, who was working as an assistant. Nobel became deeply attached to her and eventually set her up in a flat in Paris; marriage was no doubt inappropriate at the time because of their different social status. The difference of religion, too, must have been a factor.

Bertha von Suttner, Nobel's secretary in 1876 who later became well known as an ardent worker for peace.

His elder brother Ludwig, we know, strongly disapproved and urged his brother to break off the liaison. Nevertheless, it persisted for nearly twenty heart-breaking years. From the beginning, the two were totally unsuited. Alfred was a serious-minded intellectual, twice Sophie's age, preoccupied with international business matters and used to moving in high society. By contrast, Sophie—whom he sometimes referred to as the Troll—was a gay flibbertigibbet of humble origin, utterly resistant to Alfred's attempts to improve her mind and social graces and turn her into a cultivated society woman. She was wildly extravagant (though this was a fault Alfred could endure better than most men), unfaithful, and a general embarrassment. In return, Alfred was patient and, according to his own lights, understanding.

A man of different temperament might perhaps have found some compromise, but Alfred was quite out of his depth. Eventually, in 1891, she wrote to say that she had become pregnant by a young Hungarian officer. Perhaps grateful for the prospect of being relieved of his tempestuous mistress, Alfred replied kindly and settled a handsome annuity on her. Later he even visited her and the child in Vienna.

Despite this, his troubles were not over. When she did eventually marry her officer in 1895, both continued to try to extract more money from him. The persecution even continued after his death in 1896, for Sophie threatened to publish Alfred's letters to her. To avoid scandal, she was bought off by the executors. The liaison was a total disaster, and must have deepened Alfred's melancholy in his later years. History is full of "ifs", but it is interesting to imagine how different his life might have been had he made a happy marriage with an understanding and compatible wife.

7 The Will and its Consequences

On 7th December, 1896, Nobel suffered a stroke, which was to prove quickly fatal. Ragnar Sohlman, a young Swedish engineer, who had been engaged by Nobel as his personal assistant in 1893, was summoned by telegram from Bofors. However, he did not arrive at San Remo until the evening of 10th December, some hours after Nobel's death in the early hours of the same day. Too late also were two nephews—Hjalmar and Emanuel—who had also been urgently summoned. Nobel's deep forebodings had been fulfilled: he died without any "close friend or relation whose kind hand would some day close one's eyes and whisper in one's ear a gentle and sincere word of comfort."

Nobel's old friend, Nathan Söderblom, came from Paris to give a memorial address at a brief ceremony in the house at San Remo. The body was then taken to Stockholm for a formal funeral service in the cathedral, followed by cremation. His ashes were interred in the family grave in the New Cemetery in Stockholm, beside the remains of his parents and of his ill-fated brother, Emil. Throughout his life Nobel had had a curious obsession that he would be buried alive, and he expressly directed that his veins should be opened before the cremation. Perhaps this obsession was inherited. His father, too, had the same fear, and among the uses he suggested for a kind of chipboard he patented was the following rather macabre one: "For coffins, which, while combining cheapness and lightness with tasteful construction and the necessary decoration, could be so made that a person coming to life in them could lift the lid from inside, the lid being provided with airholes for breathing and with a cord attached to a bell."

Ragnar Sohlman, Nobel's personal assistant at the time of his death.

64

Testament

Jag undertecknad Alfred Bernhard Nobel förklarar härmed efter moget betänkande min yttersta vilja i afseende å den egendom jag vid min död kan efterlemna vara följande:

Öfver hela min återstående realiserbara förmögenhet förfogas på följande sätt: Kapitalet, af utredningsmännen realiseradt till säkra värdepapper, skall utgöra en fond hvars ränta årligen utdelas som prisbelöning åt dem som under det förlupne året hafva gjort menskligheten den största nytta. Räntan delas i fem lika delar som tillfalla: en del den som inom fysikens område har gjort den vigtigaste upptäckt eller uppfinning; en del den som har gjort den vigtigaste kemiska upptäckt eller förbättring; en del den som har gjort den vigtigaste upptäckt inom fysiologiens eller medicinens domän; en del den som inom literaturen har producerat det utmärktaste i idealisk rigtning; och en del åt den som har verkat mest eller best för folkens förbrödrande och afskaffande eller minskning af stående armeer samt bildande och spridande af fredskongresser. Priset för fysik och kemi utdelas af Svenska Vetenskapsakademien; för fysiologiska eller medicinska arbeten af Carolinska Institutet i Stockholm; för literatur af Akademien i Stockholm samt för fredsförfäktare af ett utskott af fem personer som väljas af Norska Stortinget. Det är min uttryckliga vilja att vid prisutdelningarne intet afseende fästes vid någon slags nationalitetstillhörighet sålunda att den värdigaste erhåller priset antingen han är Skandinav eller ej.

Detta testamente är hittills det enda giltiga och upphäfver alla mina föregående testamentariska bestämmelser om sådane skulle förefinnas efter min död.

Slutligen anordnar jag såsom dödom varande min uttryckliga önskan och vilja att efter min död pulsådrorne uppskäras och att sedan detta skett och tydliga dödstecken af kompetente läkare intygats liket förbrännes i så kallad krematorugn.

Paris den 27 November 1895

Alfred Bernhard Nobel

Meanwhile there had been surprising develop-
ments in connection with Nobel's will. On 15th
December, Sohlman was told that Nobel had
made him his executor, jointly with Rudolf
Lilljeqvist, a business associate in an electro-
chemical venture in Sweden, whom we have already
mentioned. For Sohlman, an inexperienced young
engineer still in his twenties, the news was dis-
quieting; no doubt he would have been even more
concerned had he known that the task was to involve
him in a major international legal dispute conducted
in a blaze of publicity. His consolation was that
Lilljeqvist was a much more experienced man of
business, some fourteen years his senior. For Sohlman
this was a curious twist of fate for, as we shall see,
the totally unexpected assignment was vitally to
affect the whole of his career.

For the moment, the terms of the will itself were
not known, but as soon as the full text had been
made available to Sohlman, and he had had some
preliminary legal advice, it became clear that its
execution presented grave technical difficulties.
Nobel's general intentions were clear enough: after
certain private bequests to members of his family,
the residue of his fortune was to be used for the
endowment of what we now know as the Nobel
Prizes. The will reads: "The whole of my remaining
realizable estate shall be dealt with in the following
way: The capital shall be invested by my executors
in safe securities and shall constitute a fund, the
interest on which shall be annually distributed in
the form of prizes to those who, during the preceding
year, shall have conferred the greatest benefit on
mankind. The said interest shall be divided into five
equal parts, which shall be apportioned as follows:
one part to the person who shall have made the
most important discovery or invention within the
field of physics; one part to the person who shall
have made the most important chemical dis-

covery or improvement; one part to the person who shall have made the most important discovery within the domain of physiology or medicine; one part to the person who shall have produced in the field of literature the most outstanding work of an idealistic tendency; and one part to the person who shall have done the most or the best work to promote fraternity between nations, for the abolition or reduction of standing armies and for the holding and promotion of peace congresses . . . the most worthy shall receive the prize whether he be a Scandinavian or not."

(a) Nobel Peace medal—
obverse.

(b) Nobel Peace medal—
reverse.

The prizes for science were to be awarded by the Swedish Academy of Science; those for medicine by the Caroline Institute in Stockholm; that for literature by the Academy in Stockholm; that for peace by the Norwegian Storting (Parliament). The prizes would be no trifles, for Nobel's estate was finally valued at 33 million Swedish crowns, equivalent to about £1,800,000, an immense sum in those days for a private fortune.

Above right Obverse of the Nobel medals.

Above left Reverse of the Nobel medal for Physiology and Medicine.

Left Reverse of the Nobel medal for Physics and Chemistry.

Below Reverse of the Nobel medal for Literature.

Although the younger and more inexperienced man, the main burden fell on Sohlman, who had had the most direct personal relationship with Nobel; Lilljeqvist had met him only twice. Broadly speaking, his difficulties were of three kinds. Firstly, there were the legal problems. Nobel had written his will in his own hand, in Swedish, apparently without any legal advice whatsoever. It soon became clear that it was so imprecise in some respects that the courts might set it aside if it were challenged, as it very soon became clear that it might be. For example, none of the august bodies named by Nobel as adjudicators had been consulted by him. There was no provision for reimbursing them for doing a job which would not only be a labour, however worthwhile, but would involve them in much expense. Furthermore, the mere management of such a large investment was a major task, and some special body would have to be set up for the purpose. Another major legal problem was that of Nobel's domicile at the time of his death: he had homes in Sweden, France, and Italy, and he had in fact spent very little time in Sweden during his lifetime.

A second major difficulty was the question of the "realizable assets" which were to provide funds for the prizes. At the time of his death, Nobel's fortune consisted of large holdings of roughly comparable size in Sweden, Germany, France, Britain, and Russia; there were lesser, but still very considerable, sums in Norway, Austria, and Italy. To realize some of these assets could have most unfortunate repercussions, not least for the surviving members of Nobel's family. For example, Alfred Nobel's share in the Nobel Brothers' Naphtha Company in Russia amounted to some £200,000. The publication of the will prompted rumours of a forced sale, with very adverse effects on the shares of the company, then capably managed by Alfred's nephew, Emanuel. Emanuel came under heavy pressure from the rest of his family to contest the will.

A further embarrassment to the young Sohlman was a surprisingly violent press campaign against the will, carried on with the tacit approval of certain disappointed members of the family. In all, twenty relatives would have shared the whole estate if the will had been declared invalid. It was scarcely to be wondered at that they were opposed to so large a sum being lost for the benefit of a cause in which they had no personal interest, and which was even attracting public criticism. Generally speaking the campaign was waged at a depressingly insular level. A loyal Swede, it was argued, would not have dissipated his fortune by giving prizes to foreigners. The institutions named by Nobel ought not to take on these additional imposed duties, for which, it was said, they were not fitted. The delegation of the award for peace to the Norwegian Storting was particularly unpopular, for Sweden's relations with Norway at that time were strained.

Considering his youth and inexperience, Sohlman carried out very capably the task thrust upon him. Perhaps his most important single action was to find a first-class legal expert who could advise on matters of which both he and Lilljeqvist were almost wholly ignorant. Their choice fell on Carl Lindhagen, deputy justice of the Swedish Appeal Court, and events were to prove that they could not have done better. Sohlman also established a friendly relationship with the Swedish Consul General in Paris, Gustaf Nordling, who in turn found him a capable French lawyer.

All this was achieved by the end of January 1897, within a few weeks of Nobel's death. Speed

The Stock Exchange Building, Stockholm, which houses the Nobel Library of the Swedish Academy.

was vital, for with so large a fortune at stake it was expected that an attempt would be made to prove that Nobel's home had been France. In that case, all his property in France would have been liable to French tax. If it could be established, however, that his home had been Sweden, then only strictly French securities would be liable for French tax, and the saving would be great. Unfortunately, it seemed that the executors could do nothing about the estate in France until a Swedish court had given them a necessary certificate, and this might take a long time. However, this Gordian knot was astutely cut by Gustaf Nordling who—as Swedish representative—himself provided a certificate to the effect that the executors were acting in accordance with Swedish law and practice.

Lindhagen was summoned to Paris and thereafter events moved swiftly and, in some respects, dramatically. First, they went the rounds of a number of French banks collecting various securities and documents that Nobel had deposited in them. These were accumulated in a single strongroom in Paris. Meanwhile various members of the Nobel family had arrived, clearly with the intention of getting the will set aside in the French courts. Prudence, if not strict legal ethics, suggested that it would be wise to put the securities beyond the jurisdiction of these courts, by sending them to England and Sweden.

A practical difficulty arose because the French postal service would not insure any package for more than 20,000 francs, a mere drop in the ocean in view of the sums involved. The bank of Rothschild, however, was quite used to such transactions, and offered to effect the necessary insurance provided the daily shipment did not exceed $2\frac{1}{2}$ million francs. Ragnar Sohlman tells how this sum was taken daily for a week from the bank vault to the Swedish Consulate; there the individual items were

Carl Lindhagen, the deputy justice of the Swedish Appeal Court.

recorded and packaged before being taken to the Gare du Nord in Paris for dispatch to London. To avoid attracting attention, Sohlman collected the securities himself in a cab—in which he sat with a loaded revolver in his hand in case of attempted robbery. Gustaf Nordling was a great help in all this but found himself getting increasingly embarrassed. On one occasion he was discussing with the relatives the possibility of challenging the will, knowing that in the next room Sohlman was

Nobel's house in the Avenue Malakoff, Paris.

The Nobel Institute for Physics and Chemistry, Stockholm.

parcelling up the securities to put them beyond their reach!

Nordling, therefore, insisted that the relatives be told what had happened. For some reason it was supposed that this might be done with the least upset in the course of a lavish dinner party attended by everybody concerned. Perhaps this lessened the shock to the relatives, but it was still considerable. They managed to secure an attachment order to hold what little property remained in France; the major item was Nobel's fine house in the Avenue Malakoff, though the furniture had already been removed and sold. They also sought attachment orders on property in England and Germany, but without success.

Meanwhile, events had been moving in Sweden. Test cases had been brought to see whether the estate came under the jurisdiction of Stockholm or of the County Court of Karlskoga, where the Bofors works were situated. Eventually, the matter was settled in favour of Karlskoga. This led to a decision in France that the courts there had no jurisdiction because at the time of his death Nobel had been domiciled in Sweden.

Finally, on 21st May, 1897, the Swedish government formally instructed its Attorney General to have the will declared valid. He was also to give such help as they might desire to the Swedish institutions named by Nobel as adjudicators for the prizes.

Although the tide had turned there were still many difficulties. The Norwegian Storting had early accepted responsibility for the award of the peace prize, but the Swedish institutions contained members opposed to their taking on the new duties. There was some hope that even if they did so the courts might, as a compromise, decree that the estate should be divided between the relatives and the institutions without putting any special obligations at all on the latter. A minor complication was that Nobel's reference to the "Academy in Stockholm" was too vague, and it could not in law be identified with the Swedish Academy. The Social Democrat, Hjalmar Branting—who nevertheless accepted the peace prize in 1921—bitterly criticized the choice of the Swedish Academy and declared that "it would be better to be rid of both millionaires and donations." Although the other institutions finally agreed to cooperate, subject to safeguards, the Academy of Science—after a bitter internal struggle—declined. This created an awkward situation, as was intended. The will could hardly be proved if one of the main

W. C. Röntgen (1845–1903), the discoverer of X-rays and winner of the first Nobel Prize for Physics in 1901.

76

Perscheid.

J. H. Van't Hoff (1852–1911), the Dutch pioneer of stereo-chemistry, winner of the first Nobel Prize for Chemistry.

adjudicators named in it refused to have anything at all to do with the matter. Such an attitude could only encourage the relatives to renew their efforts to have the will declared null and void.

To resolve the deadlock, it was decided to try again to reach a compromise with the relatives. As a preliminary, a meeting of all the legal advisers—from Sweden, France, Germany, and England—was held in Stockholm in the summer of 1897. All agreed that in none of these countries was any attempt to overturn the will likely to succeed. The position was put to the family, and although they lodged a further protest, the inventory of Nobel's estate was finally submitted to the Karlskoga Court on 9th November 1897, nearly a year after

E. A. von Behring (1854–1917), who won the first Nobel Prize for Medicine for his work in the field of immunization.

his death. Eventually, death duty was agreed at about £200,000. It was then possible to begin to dispose of appropriate assets and realize the estate to provide an endowment fund for the prizes.

Meanwhile, some of the disappointed relatives had fallen out among themselves. In December 1897 Emanuel Nobel invited Ragnar Sohlman to spend a few days with him in St. Petersburg for friendly discussion about the disposal of Nobel's Russian assets, especially his share in The Nobel Brothers' Naphtha Company, whose fortunes were still suffering from the uncertainty. A solution was reached, subject to the agreement of the Swedish branch of the family.

It looked, however, as though this would not

R. F. A. Sully-Prudhomme (1839–1907), the French poet who won the first Nobel Prize for Literature.

be forthcoming, for in February 1898 they started formal legal action to fight the will. It was to be a big case, for the defendants were not only the executors but the Swedish government, the Norwegian Storting, and the three adjudicating institutions.

Fortunately, the involvement of the Norwegian Storting caused a delay in the hearing, and in the meantime better judgement prevailed; a settlement was reached out of court in the summer of 1898. Under its terms, the relatives agreed to accept the general conditions of the will, and forego any claim on the residual estate which was to fund the prizes. In return, they were to receive the interest earned by the assets in 1897, a sizeable sum. It was also agreed that a member of Robert Nobel's family should be consulted when the prize rules were drawn up. A powerful factor was the attitude of Emanuel Nobel, who had always been a moderating influence. At the very outset, in San Remo, he had reminded the young Sohlman that in Russia the executor of a will is known as *Dushe Prikashshik*—the "spokesman for the soul." For his part he had always wanted to respect his uncle's wishes, so far as the obscurities of the will allowed.

As the legal dust of the family dispute began to settle, the Royal Academy of Sciences announced that it too would join discussions about the award of the prizes. Although many formalities had still to be completed, the agreement in principle of all the

J. H. Dunant (1828–1910), the Swiss philanthropist who inspired the foundation of the International Red Cross, and who shared the first peace prize with F. Passy.

81

parties meant that it was now possible to consider the final objective, the setting up of permanent organizations to give effect to Nobel's wishes with regard to the prizes. To make sure that the claims of all candidates were properly examined, and the money properly invested, it was necessary to set up considerable administrative machinery. In the end it was decided to set up a Nobel Foundation of

F. Passy (1822–1912), the French economist and author, who shared the first Nobel Prize for Peace.

five members, with deputies. The chairman was to be appointed by the Swedish government and the other members by the prize-awarding institutions. Money was set aside for a headquarters, and to cover the expenses of the prize juries.

Not until the turn of the century, however, was all this done. The proposed statutes were approved by the Swedish government in the summer of 1900. On 25th September of that year the trustees met for the first time, and Alfred Nobel's intention had at last been achieved. One of the first tasks of the Board of the Foundation was to appoint from their own members an executive director. Appropriately, and almost inevitably, their choice was Ragnar Sohlman, whose determination and single-minded purpose had done so much to bring about the desired end in face of all the obstacles.

The first prizes were awarded in Stockholm in 1901. The presentation was made by the Crown Prince of Sweden before a distinguished international gathering which included Emanuel Nobel and other members of the family. Each prize was worth £8,000, in those days a very handsome sum indeed. The recipients of the scientific and medical awards were W. C. Röntgen, of Germany, pioneer of X-rays; J. H. van't Hoff, of Holland, famous for his work on stereochemistry; and E. A. von Behring, of Germany, discoverer of antitoxins and pioneer of their use in the treatment of diphtheria. The prize for literature went to R. F. A. Sully-Prudhomme, of France, and the peace prize was shared between J. H. Dunant, of Switzerland, and F. Passy, of France.

This glittering ceremony has since been repeated every year, except for the war years, and some 300 of the world's most intellectually gifted men (and women) have benefited from Nobel's generosity. Today, each prize is of greater value but, especially in science and medicine, it is commonly shared between two or three prizewinners. To a great extent, this reflects the fact that in these fields progress depends more on brilliant teamwork than on individual genius, a development that might not have had Nobel's approval. The dignified formality of the proceedings makes it hard to remember that they arose from controversy and strife. Perhaps it is appropriate that this should have been so. As Nobel was a controversial figure in his lifetime, so he remained controversial in the fulfilment of his wishes after his death.

Nobel's tomb.

NOBEL

Date Chart

c. 500 B.C. Inflammable materials began to be used in military engagements.

c. 7th century A.D.
    "Greek Fire" used by the Byzantines.

c. 11th century A.D.
    Chinese discover inflammable qualities of saltpetre.

13th century A.D.

1346   Roger Bacon describes gunpowder.
    Battle of Crécy, first important European battle in which gunpowder was used.

1376   Explosive shells probably used by Venetians at Battle of Jadra.

1618–48   Thirty Years' War, rifles used extensively for first time.

1761   Birth of Henry Shrapnel, inventor of the shrapnel shell.

1799   Birth of C. F. Schönbein, discoverer of guncotton.

c. 19th century A.D.
    Introduction of breech-loaded shells.

c. 19th century A.D.

1803   Introduction of percussion cap.
    Shrapnel shells officially approved for use by British Army.

1807   Birth of T. J. Pelouze, distinguished French chemist under whom Nobel worked briefly.

1812   Birth of Ascanio Sobrero, discoverer of nitroglycerine.

1827   Birth of Sir Frederick Abel, British explosives expert.

1833	Birth of Alfred Nobel.
1842	Immanuel Nobel and his family move to Moscow.
1845	Discovery of guncotton.
1846	Guncotton patented in England.
1847	Discovery of the explosive, nitroglycerine. 21 killed in explosion at guncotton factory, Kent.
c. 1850–52	Alfred Nobel in the U.S.
1854–56	Crimean War; Immanuel Nobel's mines used by Russian forces.
1863	Immanuel Nobel manufacturing new form of gunpowder.
1863	Nitroglycerine factory established by Immanuel and Alfred Nobel.
1864	Death of Emil Nobel in explosion at the Nobel nitroglycerine factory.
1865	First high-explosives factory established near Stockholm.
1865	Nobel's first factory outside Sweden established at Krümmel, near Hamburg.
c. 1865	Discovery of a smokeless gunpowder by J. F. Schulze.
1866	Krümmel factory destroyed in explosion.
1867	Dynamite patented.
1868	The Giant Powder Co., San Francisco, first American venture in high explosives.
1869	Act of Parliament severely to restrict use of nitroglycerine or preparations containing it in Britain.
1872	Death of Immanuel Nobel, Alfred's father.
1875	Alfred Nobel addresses Society of Arts, London.

1875	Blasting gelatine perfected.
1877	The Nobel Brothers' Naphtha Co. formed in Russia.
1888	Nobel introduces ballistite.
1891	Nobel leaves France to live in Italy.
1892	Berne Peace Congress impresses Nobel.
1893–95	High Court case in Britain over infringement of the ballistite/cordite patent.
1893	Nobel decides to leave part of fortune as prize for promotion of world peace.
1896	Death of Nobel.
1897	Nobel's will declared valid by the Swedish courts.
1900	Board of Nobel Foundation formed under Nobel's will for administration of the prizes.
1901	First Nobel Prizes awarded.

Glossary

Bacillus A type of bacterium. Some bacilli cause disease.

Ballistite A mixture of nitrocotton (*q.v.*) and nitro-glycerine (*q.v.*) which burns well and is a good propellant.

Blasting Gelatine A mixture basically of nitro-glycerine (*q.v.*) and nitrocellulose (*q.v.*) per-fected by Nobel in 1875; relatively stable, its explosiveness can be varied by altering the proportion of the two ingredients.

Breech The back part of a gun barrel.

Cellulose An organic compound of carbon, hydrogen and oxygen which forms the solid framework of plants. It is sometimes fibrous, and if cotton and other forms of nearly pure cellulose are treated with nitric acid (*q.v.*), a very highly explosive product, guncotton (*q.v.*), is formed.

Charcoal The black residue of charred wood. It is a form of carbon.

Cordite A smokeless explosive similar to ballistite (*q.v.*), but with the addition of some acetone and petroleum jelly to make it more stable. It can be extruded in the form of cords and, if desired, chopped into pellets.

Dynamite A highly explosive but relatively safe mix-ture of nitroglycerine (*q.v.*) and kieselguhr (*q.v.*) patented by Nobel in 1867.

Ethyl Alcohol (C_2H_5OH) The stimulant in wine, beer and spirits. It is used in many chemical reactions.

Explosive A substance which, on ignition by friction, detonation, etc., undergoes very rapid decomposi-tion with the release of a large amount of energy.

Fuse A slow-burning cord used to set off a bomb, blasting charge, etc.

Greek Fire A mixture of inflammable materials, the principal one probably being naphtha (*q.v.*), used by the Byzantines in the defence of their Empire.

Guncotton A highly explosive material produced by nitrating cotton, or some other form of nearly pure cellulose (*q.v.*) with nitric acid (*q.v.*).

Gunpowder An explosive mixture of saltpetre (*q.v.*), charcoal (*q.v.*) and sulphur (*q.v.*).

High Explosives Term usually used for the various nitro-compounds, as distinct from gunpowder.

Kieselguhr A very porous form of clay which, mixed with nitroglycerine (*q.v.*), produces dynamite.

Methyl Alcohol (CH_3OH) Form of alcohol closely related to ethyl alcohol (*q.v.*).

Muzzle Open end of a firearm.

Muzzle-loader Type of firearm that is loaded through the muzzle (*q.v.*).

Naphtha An inflammable hydrocarbon.

Nitrate Salt given by combining nitric acid (*q.v.*) with an inorganic base or an alcohol.

Nitrocellulose Guncotton (*q.v.*).

Nitroglycerine ($C_2H_5(ONO_2)_3$) Extremely explosive oily liquid made by treating glycerine with nitric acid.

Percussion Cap Small copper cap or cylinder in a firearm, used to detonate the main charge when struck by a hammer.

Rifling Spiral grooving on the inside of the barrel of a firearm; it spins the bullet and so gives greater accuracy.

Saltpetre (KNO_3) A white crystalline salt used in the making of gunpowder; potassium nitrate.

Shrapnel Explosive shell filled with small iron missiles; named after its inventor Henry Shrapnel (1761–1842).

Sobrero's Process The production of nitroglycerine (*q.v.*) by treating glycerine with nitric acid (*q.v.*). This process formed the basis of Nobel's high explosives factory in Winterwick.

Sulphur Pale yellow, non-metallic element used in the making of gunpowder (*q.v.*).

Touch-hole Small hole in firearm where the light was applied to ignite the charge and fire the weapon.

Further Reading

It is hoped that this brief life of Alfred Nobel will stimulate a desire to know more about this remarkable man and the prizes he founded. For this purpose the following works will prove helpful.

Schück, H. and Sohlman, R., *The Life of Alfred Nobel* (London, Heinemann, 1929). An authoritative work. Henrik Schück was a chairman of the Nobel Foundation; Ragnar Sohlman was the executor of Nobel's will and the first executive director of the Foundation.

Bergengren, E., *Alfred Nobel: The man and his work* (Nelson, 1962). This is similar in scope to the above, but is less reticent about Nobel's private life. (Translated from the Swedish.)

Schück, H., Sohlman, R., Österling, A., Liljestrand, G., Westgren, A., Siegbahn, M., Schon, A., and Stähle, N. K., (edited by the Nobel Foundation), *Nobel: The man and his prizes* (Elsevier, 1962). This book was originally published in 1950 to mark the jubilee of the Nobel Foundation. The edition listed above includes the original work and brings the story of the prizes up to 1961. It is an important source book. The greater part consists of accounts of the prize-winners and their work, but in addition there is a short biography of Nobel, the story of the creation of the Foundation, and an account of the Foundation's administration, finances, and statutes.

Hennig, R., *Alfred Nobel: Der Erfinder des Dynamits und Gründer der Nobelstiftung* (Stuttgart, *c.* 1912). A small book, mainly of interest for its illustrations of early explosives works.

Les Prix Nobel en 1901, etc. From 1901, the Nobel Foundation has issued an annual volume to mark the presentation ceremony. Each consists mainly of short biographies of the prize-winners and (after the first volume) summaries of their Nobel lectures delivered in Stockholm. The first volume contains a short biography of Alfred Nobel by P.-T. Cleve.

Nobel Prize Lectures. Peace. Vol. 1 (1901–1925); Vol. 2 (1926–1950); Vol. 3 (1951–1970). Physics. Vol. 1 (1901–1921); Vol. 2 (1922–1941); Vol. 3 (1942–1963); Vol. 4 (1963–1970). Chemistry. Vol. 1 (1901–1921); Vol. 2 (1922–1941); Vol. 3 (1942–1962); Vol. 4 (1963–1970). Physiology or Medicine. Vol. 1 (1901–1921); Vol. 2 (1922–1941); Vol. 3 (1942–1962); Vol. 4 (1963–1970). Literature. Vol. 1 (1901–1967) (Elsevier). These volumes, part of a continuing series, give the full texts of the lectures given in Stockholm by the laureates on the awarding of their prizes.

EXPLOSIVES. A technical account of the development of nitrocellulose and nitroglycerine explosives in the 19th century, together with a bibliography, is given by J. McGrath in *A History of Technology*, Vol. V, edited by Charles Singer, E. J. Holmyard, A. R. Hall, and Trevor I. Williams (Oxford University Press, 1958).

Guttmann, O., *The Manufacture of Explosives* (London, 1895).

Marshall, A., *Explosives* (Churchill, 1917). Designed primarily for the use of the explosives manufacturer, but it includes much interesting historical information.

Index

Abel, Frederick, 17, 35
Acetone, use of, 36
Aircraft, Nobel's interest in, 48
Alcohol, ethyl, 34
Alcohol, methyl, 31
Andrée, S. A., 48
Artillery, introduction of, 14
Aurora Lamp Oil Company, 24
Avigliana munitions factory, 37

Bacon, Roger, 13
Baku, 44, 46
Ballistite, 34, 35, 37
Barbe, Paul, 40
Behring, E. A. von, 83
Björkborn, 50
Blasting gelatine, 32
Bofors-Gullspräng Company, 49, 64, 76

Camphor, use of in explosives, 35
Constantinople, siege of, 14
Cordite, 36, 58
Crimean War, 20

Detonator, invention of, 26
Dewar, James, 36
Dunant, J. H., 83
Du Pont de Nemours, 42
Dynamite, 31, 33

Electrochemistry, 47
Ericcson, John, 24
Ether, use of in explosives, 34
Explosives Commission (UK), 36

Firearms, introduction of, 14

Greek Fire, 13
Guncotton (nitrocellulose), 17, 32, 33, 34, 35
Gunpowder, 13, 15, 26, 33, 42

Heleneborg factory, 27

Johnson, D., 33

Kieselguhr, 31
Krümmel factory, 29

Lamp oil, 47
Lilljeqvist, Rudolf, 47, 67, 69, 71
Lindhagen, Carl, 71, 72

Nemesis, 58
Nitroglycerine, 17, 26, 27, 28, 29, 31, 32, 34, 35
Nobel, Alfred
—early experiments with nitro-glycerine, 26
—disaster at Heleneborg, 27
—invention of detonator, 26
—invention of dynamite, 31
—introduces ballistite, 35
—Cordite Case, 37
—Russian petroleum industry, 46
—loneliness of, 52, 54
—interest in poetry, 57, 61
—Peace Movement, 59, 60
—and Bertha von Suttner, 61, 62
—and Sophie, 62, 63
—death of, 64
—disputed will of, 67, 69–83
Nobel Brothers Naphtha Company, 46, 70, 79
Nobel, Carolina (née Ahlsell), 19
Nobel Dynamite Trust, 40
Nobel, Emil, 19, 23, 27
Nobel, Emanuel, 64, 70, 79, 83
Nobel Foundation, 82
Nobel, Hjalmar, 64
Nobel, Immanuel, 19, 20, 21, 24, 26, 27, 28

Nobel, Ludwig, 19, 23, 24, 43, 44, 46, 47, 63
Nobel, Robert, 19, 23, 40, 43, 44, 81
Nordling, Gustaf, 71, 72, 74, 75

Panama Scandal, 41
Passy, F., 83
Patent Bacillus, 58
Peace Congress (1892), 60
Pelouze, T. J., 24, 26
Percussion cap, 15
Petroleum, 43, 44, 47
Pipelines, introduction of, 45
Poetry, Nobel's interest in, 57, 58, 61
Poudre B, 34
Prizes, Nobel, 9, 67, 68, 70, 76, 82, 83

Reid, W. F., 33
Rifles, 15, 34, 43
Röntgen, W. C., 83
Rothschild (bankers), 72
Rubber, synthetic, 47
Rudbeck, Olaf, 18, 19

St. Petersburg, Nobel family's interests in, 20, 24, 25, 43, 44, 79
San Francisco, 29
San Remo, 38, 50, 81
Schönbein, C. F., 17
Schultze, J. F. E., 33
Shaffner, T. P., 42
Shelley, influence on Nobel, 58, 59
Smokeless powder, 33
Sobrero, Ascanio, 17, 25, 26, 28
Société Centrale de Dynamite, 40, 41
Society of Arts, 31, 33

Söderblom, Nathan, 58, 64
Sohlman, Ragnar, 64, 67, 69, 71, 72, 79, 83
Storting (Norwegian Parliament), 68, 70, 76, 80
Sully-Prudhomme, R. F. A., 83
Suttner, Bertha von (*née* Kinsky), 60, 61, 62

Swedish Academy of Science, 68, 76, 81

Tankers, introduction of, 45, 57

Uppsala University, 19

Van't Hoff, J. H., 83

Vieille, P. M. E., 34, 38

Will, Alfred Nobel's, 67, 68, 76, 78, 79
Winterwick factory, 28, 29

Zinin, Nikolai, 20, 25

Picture Credits

The author and publisher wish to thank all those who have given permission for illustrations to be used on the following pages: A. B. Bofors, 49, 50, 51; 60–61; The British Petroleum Company, 47; Du Pont de Nemours International S.A., 41; Mary Evans Picture Library, 11, 12–13, 15, 21, 23, 24, 25, 34, 35, 38, 39, 43, 44, 46, 48, 59, 62, 80; I.C.I. Ltd., 28–29, 30; Keystone Press Agency, 8, 10; The Nobel Foundation, Stockholm, *frontispiece*, 16, 18, 19, 22, 27, 33, 53, 54, 55, 56, 65, 66, 68, 69, 73, 74, 85; Paul Popper Ltd., 71, 75, 77; The Radio Times Hulton Picture Library, 32, 36, 45; The Royal Institution of Great Britain, 78, 79, 81, 82.